Southern & Conservative

Rosa's Concepts

Soldier, American flag, and a baby

Rosa Ann Crowder

2

ISBN: 9781070859071

"I want what you want. I want a town that is thriving, safe, and full of opportunities for our children and us. As a business owner, I know what it takes to bring in business and grow our economy. As a mother, I know what it's like to want a safe and prosperous environment to raise your kids. I know that it is up to us, working together if we are going to make these things happen." – Rosa Ann Crowder

Table of Contents

I Support President Donald Trump

Make America Great Again!

The United States of America has never had a President like President Donald Trump. We probably never will again. I think at this time in our crazy world, we need a man like Donald Trump to be our President.

President Trump is not politically correct, and he is tough! In my opinion, Donald Trump is perfect!

There are those trying to bring him down, and he still will take on the fight! No, he's not perfect but what President ever was! Being tough is precisely what's needed today!

No other president has had to put up with what our President is enduring every day. We need to support him and help him return America to what America used to be.

There are even some Republicans who should be ashamed. We should all be supporting our President.

Best President Ever

I think many people cannot see beyond Donald Trump's personality and look at what his policies have done for America.

I think that President Donald Trump looks at America and sees so many systems that need significant overhauls. Many areas left broken by the previous administration, and he is trying to tackle as many as possible.

Obama left him a broken economy, military, VA, foreign policy, unfair trade policies, broken borders, and immigration policies and demoralized law enforcement.

Donald Trump is the hardest working president in my lifetime. He never stops, and he has to fight the lying media and the elitist politicians in both parties every step of the way.

Furthermore, Trump looks at his job like a business, and he is trying to correct what is broken. He is not and will never be a slick talking politician like Obama was. His only goal is to fix things.

Sometimes I get into discussions with people who only want to talk about Trump's temperament or personality. I do not waste much time with those who know nothing about his policies.

When people call you a racist because you support Trump, it speaks more to their character than yours. They are usually telling you how ignorant of the facts they are.

Sometimes you have to consider the source.

White House

I would hate to think what the condition of this country would be if Donald Trump weren't in the White House.

May the Lord give him wisdom, strength, good health, and protect him as he continues to serve the American people at such a significant cost to him personally as well as his family.

- ❏ President Trump is truly a blessing for America.

- ❏ God Bless President Trump, and God Bless America!

- ❏ Pray for our President!

Wake-up America

Build "The Wall"

We should thank, President Trump, for building a military wall of protection on our SOUTHERN border. We are parents who love our children. Murder, pedophilia and human trafficking are on the rise as well as disease.

We must protect our children. Even companies require applications to be filled out and some require a medical examination before accepting applicants. The United States must require the same of ALL IMMIGRANTS.

Stop Killing Babies

Abortion in America is on the rise. Why do baby murderers attempt to convince themselves & everyone else that killing their child is the right thing to do?

Also, why are liberals being trained to kill off the American population, while at the same time allowing millions of immigrants & Muslims into our country who generally do not abort their children?

"The number of undocumented immigrant children in United States government administration custody has surpassed 14,000, a rise that displays no signs of decreasing as the Trump administration attempts to force policies that are holding them in government facilities longer."

www.sfchronicle.com/author/tal-kopan/

Unauthorized Immigrant Settlement

(written October 2018

Most Unauthorized Immigrant Settlement Happens When They Overstay Their Visas. How Can The Immigrants Be Stopped?

The only time Americans come together was when threatened as a whole. The remainder of the time, we fought amongst ourselves. We are being attacked from the inside out from our politicians from both parties. And the press is eating it up.

I think we all agree that the reality of life in Central America - Guatemala, Honduras, and El Salvador are dangerous places to live. Because of threats and repression from the governing party of President Juan Orlando Hernandez.

However, no other country would allow a caravan of migrants to enter their country, and we as American can not let it. Not a single decent person in this Nation would ever want to see any force used.

At the same time, we no longer have a Country, if people from all corners believe they can force their way into this Country.

Like a Hollywood movie, anyone neutral can recognize what is practical, realistically possible, and what is a make-believe based narrative.

The caravan journey of refugees from Honduras is the media's latest venture into fictional reporting. The photos the media uses are nothing more than scene shots. The situation isn't right, anyway, you look at it.

We are amazed at individuals who run in marathons. Those who hike a long distance by foot. Those few who have cycled across America, and so forth for support of a charity or a cause. Do you believe it is a journey you could make?

A 3000-mile trip requires training preparation and support. These athletes have support vehicles that follow them to carry supplies of snacks, water, places to rest and provide care to the athletes.

I believe that most people in reasonable shape can walk 25 miles a day if they push themselves. The next day they would likely be too sore from standing though. It would be highly unlikely they could walk 25 miles the next day.

Rodrigo Abeja is one of the caravan's leaders. In his words, "We don't yet know if we will make it to the (U.S.) border, but we are going to keep going as far as we can." (source: National Post)

This caravan averaged more than 100 miles per day. In and of itself, this distance traveled should make the story questionable. It just makes no sense whatsoever.

People require food and water. Just for basic survival, a group this size would need several truckloads of snacks and water per day. What does make sense to me is that somebody or a group of people within the United States put this caravan into motion.

"Mexicans join the march. By joining an organized group which included refugees, Mexican nationals have a greater chance of entering the U.S. Mexican, and Honduran marchers are holding flags."
Source: San Francisco Examiner

There should be no conjecture that some of the travelers are gang members. MS-13 has made a horrifying impact on life for those living in Central America. They have also been sneaking into the U.S. often.

Therefore blending in within groups of migrants allows them the cover needed to breach American territory successfully. Many try to swim across.

This caravan of migrants has some options to travel. One way of travel is to the nearest crossing point in Texas that would have the group moving through a risky and dangerous territory. Another direction of travel is by a more natural trail to the California border.

It makes sense to me that the gang members and terrorists enter through the California border while the more prominent groups try to come through Texas.

Democrats blame Republicans and Republicans blame Democrats. Each believes the other is trying to influence the outcome of the midterm elections.

It is unlikely either party are involved, but it does make an ethical conspiracy theory. There are flaws in both arguments, but that does not mean third parties are not acting on their own to influence the elections.

As long as American employers are willing to hire illegal workers, and the government does not crack down on the process, more will come in search of employment.

Am I Guilty Of My Heritage?

Really? What's Next?

What "Isn't" Considered Racist and Offensive These Days?

The moment you are born white, you instantly become a racist? I have had enough of apologizing for being white and a conservative. God chose to make us who we are - he chose our color. IMAGINE THAT?

You do not need to apologize to anyone. No one gets to decide what color in which are born. Just ridiculous. If you are upset about the color of my skin, then blame GOD.....because it is HIS fault......

Today everything is racist. That card is "so overplayed" it means nothing. I swear grass is racist because it's green. Some people don't know the real meaning of the word anymore. They are trying to read into what is not there.

The ONLY discriminating going on here is an agenda to get God out of our minds and lives. It is a leftist group creating a prejudice that doesn't exist. This ridiculous and laughable.

God's teachings say we are all God's children and should love one another as brothers and sisters.

These idiots believe everything is racism... Good grief! People out there think that EVERYTHING is "racist"! It's getting there is nothing politically correct about this, Nothing at all.

If anyone is continuing to push racism in America, it's them. It is more proof of my belief that there are people who see racism in everything.

I have friends of all races, and you know what? I'm not ashamed of that fact. I'm not ashamed, and I never will be embarrassed, of being white either. I'm not guilty of my heritage.

It is nothing more than reverse judgment - discrimination, and honestly, they can shove it. If you do not like me cause I am white? Cool. You are racist! Now, go pick on another white Christian.

For supper last night, I ate tomatoes, carrots, zucchini, and potatoes, with onions. So tomorrow, I POOP BROWN, yep, I must be racist. Alternatively, let's call it DIGESTION. VEGETABLES are good to eat.

Just as an Asian is born Asian and a black woman is born a black woman, I was born a white female (pretty sure that's not a choice I had)

I have come to a conclusion, there's a 30-year-old liberal hate-monger, living in his or her parent's basement, playing video games & eating fruit loops, who is being paid to hunt this stuff up!

It seems like everything you say or do (see or hear) has a racial or sexist spin on it.

Hate-mongering groups over analyzed

Anyone can twist things to be racist! It seems like anything, and everything you say do you see or hear has some racial or Sexist over-tone to it.

It is rubbish like this that keeps racism alive and well. Someone is always stirring the pot about sexism and racism!

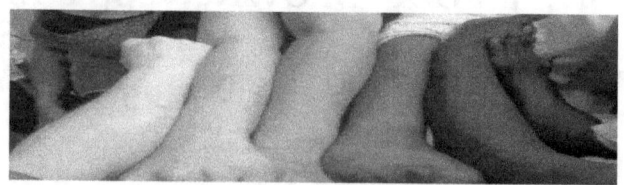

Only in America - The American Way - Crime and Politics

United States of America

- Pharmacies make the sick walk all the way to the rear of the store to get a prescription while healthy people can purchase cigarettes at the front.

- People request a diet coke with their double cheeseburgers and a large fry.

- Banks leave entries open and then secure the pens to the counters.

- We have cars worth thousands of dollars in the driveway and leave useless junk in the garage.

- We use voicemail to monitor calls.

- We have call waiting, so we do not miss a call from someone we did not want to communicate with, in the first place.

- We buy hot dogs in packs of ten and the buns in packages of eight.

- We have homeless people dwelling under bridges, in the woods, and on the back roads; our veterans are getting short-changed; while lawmakers, criminals, and politicians are filling their pockets.

"I think we live in a love-starved nation. Everywhere you go there are apparently people who have not had the proper kind of love in their lives." Joyce Meyer

Corruption - What Can We Do

I strongly feel that we can make a difference. We need to take a closer look at our education system. Parents, grandparents, churches, and teachers of our society commit to helping in redeveloping beautiful minds in our children.

Then we will have a chance to become a nation that is corruption free.

For me, the labor movement and public education, linked as the essential building blocks, we will have a stronger middle class and a path to the American dream.

I think we must seek Jesus Christ in promoting peace within America as well as "World Peace." We must acquire an individual relationship with Jesus Christ.

Then we all could understand that for us to keep the peace that we must first learn to seek "Jesus Christ" daily with knowing that peace within.

The American Dream -

The Illegal Way

Illegal Drugs and Prescription Abuse

It seems to me that organized crime in America is more organized than our law enforcement. Corruption is the enemy.

It takes a toll on us, our relationships, our friends, and especially our children. But how can we get rid of corruption?

Organized crime in America saw and understood that 'working within the system' was a pointless exercise and therefore not a viable option to realize the American Dream.

Organized crime in America takes in over a billion dollars a year and spends very little on taxes, insurance, employees, and office supplies.

Criminals start out small, and their activities get larger than themselves. Therefore, they acquire cheap labor.

Immigrant labor is primarily responsible for the success of the industrialization of the preparation and sale of illegal drugs, weapons, etc.

Also, we have corrupted police officers and crooked politicians. What can we do?

Socialism

When people get too comfortable

They stop caring and get disconnected.

Throbbing with life, dispelling all dismay

Wanting recognition for their victory

A success that has not yet achieved

Social justice is not all cut and dry.

It opens up a world of possibilities.

Causes too many storms for tomorrow

Civilization gets destroyed

It is like putting a square in a circle.

Is Organized Crime and Politics the Same Thing?

Is Our Justice System a Joke?

Take A Stand! FIX HERE FIRST!

When there is a debate, there are answers. If there is no sharing of power, no control of law, no responsibility; there is injustice, bribery, subjugation, and resentment.

Take care of our own FIRST!!! Our veterans and our elderly and pensions and child welfare and disabled BEFORE FOREIGN AID

Our nation is in debt up to the eyeballs; we have homeless people everywhere. We have children who are starving because their parents are on meth and other drugs. Too many children are neglected and abused.

The Elderly can't get their medicine. Our Veterans have been "short-changed" all around. Pensioners forced to work far too long. Our disabled are refused pensions when it is evident they are in need.

Domestic violence is FAR too common Drug abuse has its share of effects, causing significant problems in society. Also, our hospitals need extra funding.

"The obstacles we face today – poverty and destruction at home, war and starvation abroad – will continue to last as long as we continue to rely on the very legislators who formed them in the first place." — Donald Trump

President Donald Trump's Promises

"So to every American, in every single city near and far away, whether small or large, understand these words: You will nevermore be ignored again. Your voice, your dreams, and your hopes will determine our American destiny. And your courage, determination, goodness, and love will endlessly guide us along the way."
Donald Trump

"We will make America strong again. We will make America proud again. We will make America safe again. And we will make America great again." — Donald Trump

Conclusion - You cannot increase wealth by cutting it.

You cannot force the poor into independence by legislating the prosperous out of their freedom. What one person takes without working for, another person must work and pay taxes.

The governments cannot give money or supplements to anybody that the system does not "first" take away from somebody else.

What if, half of the people living in America, have the impression that they do not have to work. Because the opposite half is going to support them?

What if the working half gets the concept that it does no good to struggle and work hard because lazy people are going to get part of what they worked for?

I am afraid that things are just going to head in a direction that is going to be almost impossible to recover from. And, that will roughly be the end of The United States of America.

I believe that our government must lower the "debt limits." Debt has to be changed, it is out of control. Not just Americans but world-wide needs to be concerned. We have to create jobs here in America, and the cost of living needs to stay put.

America, The Beautiful, Red, White, and Blue

Using Common Sense For A Better Tomorrow

America, America aren't we tired of our government not using common sense? We have all this diversity among our government as well as among us. It doesn't matter what state we're from or whom we praise.

In reality, we are at this time separated because of greed, different religious beliefs, political opinions, and pure laziness. That should be the reason that the words "common sense" comes into play.

Then, we could sit down and have discussions about anything; concerning this part of the earth in which we live better known as "America, The Beautiful –Red, White, and Blue - The Land of The Free."

We could build even greater empires and programs together. And then everyone could survive - not too much of a problem that we could not easily adjust.

What reasons do we have for diversity? Everybody set in their ways. Everybody has their own opinion, their way of communicating, different habits, different food preferences, different ideas of sharing, and shows affection differently.

Generations remain connected by passing along their gradations, customs, and expressions or sayings for hundreds of years.

The theory of seeking "World Peace" has been in existence for thousands of years. It's time that our generation learns from the past and use common sense.

I believe that our culture is indeed unique and unconventional in our way; however, I also think we have several standard links. One link is to create unison within America.

We must seek Jesus Christ in promoting peace within America as well as "World Peace." We must develop a personal relationship with Jesus Christ.

Then we all could understand that for us to keep the peace that we must first learn to seek "Jesus Christ" daily with knowing "that peace within

Be A Soldier

America, America, Can You See Clearly

We have turned away from our duty.

This great nation, we held so dearly.

For freedom is what we will grieve.

We must defeat the immoral few.

Heading the wrong way, I fear.

America the beautiful red, white, and blue1

America, America can you see clearly?

The Armed Forces who fight to keep us free

Also, swear an oath as warriors true.

They defend our nation that we cherish so dear,

Protecting the lives of you and me

They are real heroes, young, brave and true.

Fighting to protect our flag, the red, white
and blue

America, America, open your eyes so you can
see

Terrified in ways that I never knew

The American Spirit I wish to achieve

Standing for what is right is long overdue.

Standing for what is right will not be a breeze.

I wish it could be more comfortable for the
people here.

America the beautiful red, white, and blue

"It is time to remember that old wisdom our soldiers will never forget: that whether we are black or brown or white, we all bleed the same red blood of patriots, we all enjoy the same glorious freedoms, and we all salute the same great American Flag." Donald Trump

Only in America - Southern Pride

The Removal of the Confederate Flag

To me, the Confederate Battle Flag stands for "Slavery & Freedom." Some people say that the Confederate Flag is a symbol of hate, but that is not the truth.

It was stated removing it from the Statehouse would bring peace and start a healing process, that is not true either.

Occasionally a material issue such as our heritage flag - battle flag, there are a diversity of opinions and their conditions. It is a topic of interest in our society that will last forever.

Since they removed the flag, there has only been more hatred. Shooting at someone's home because they have the flag in their yard or whatever is not a healing process.

So where is our Government now? Not publicly denouncing these acts of violence.

There is sufficient difference in the states of the Battle Flag. In the manners and habits of the people of the different parts of the United States.

Hate is terrible not only for America but the whole world. People wanted the flag down its down, let people live their life as they choose and you live yours.

The Southern Way

Confederate Flag, Grits, and Sweet Tea

No one alive today was wronged by slavery. And all the hate both ways is just a way to be racist, forget it and be a real person and look forward not back. No one can change the past? It happened. Get over it and quit making excuses.

The Confederate Flag is part of being Southern. Grits, sweet tea, and our accent is part of being Southern. It represents our region of America, our culture, and our southern charm.

It's open to both races, a variety of ethnic groups and people who move to the south.

Love the flag, keep the culture and heritage alive. Just don't emulate the low-class behavior. It's the hate in people's heart that needs to be removed.

- Confederate Flag Stands for Freedom - Land of the Free

- It is the Southern Way - It is freedom - It is our culture - It is our history.

Flags of the Confederate States of America

It is thought-provoking when one mentions the Confederate Flag, usually what comes up in our mind is the Confederate Battle flag.

However, there were several Confederate States of America Flags, five major Southern flags.

Three successive designs which served as the national flag of the Confederacy during its existence.

- Bonnie Blue Flag - which was a standard blue flag. It had only one star, and it was in the center.

The Bonnie Blue flag was the unauthorized flag of the Confederate States of America.

Even though this flag was never officially adopted, it was an uncommonly well-known favorite flag.

"We Are a Band of Brothers," is an 1861 marching song, written about the Bonnie Blue Flag, associated with the Confederate States.

The words, drafted by the Ulster-Scots entertainer Harry McCarthy, with the melody taken from the song "The Irish Jaunting Car."

- Stars And Bars - is known as the first "National Flag," which is sometimes called the Stars and Bars. "The Stars and Bars" looked almost identical to the "Stars and Stripes," and there was a conflict.

- Stainless Banner - was the second "National Flag," It just had a logo in the upper left-hand corner, and it was white and made out of silk.

- The only dilemma with the stainless banner was it sometimes looked like a flag of surrender.

- Stainless Banner - the third "National Flag" and it was the very stainless banner, but had a regular red stripe all the way down, and that is flying today. It was adequately adopted, but very few of them issued.

- Confederate Battle Flag - as we remember it. Interestingly, the first four flags are rarely spoken against. That is because most people don't even know about their legacy, and are mindlessly unaware of them.

In today's world, there is conflict about our Confederate Flags, and as a consequence, it is the Confederate Battle Flag that catches most of the hostility.

The flag was operated by the government until government officials decided to take it down, some got burned. But can be flown by citizens of the South and any parts of the United States of America.

A Little Bit of History - Wikipedia

African-American history started in the 16th century, with people from West Africa forcibly taken and sold as slaves to Spanish America.

In the 17th century, West African people were forced to English colonies in North America, and they were sold as slaves.

After the founding of the United States, colored people continued to be enslaved. Due in large part to notions of white supremacy, about four million were denied freedom from bondage and handled as being second-class people.

The Naturalization Act of 1790; United States citizenship was to whites only, and only white men of property could vote.

Reconstruction changed those circumstances and the development of the black community. Blacks participation in the great military was a conflict of the United States.

The removal of racial segregation, and the Civil Rights Movement, which sought political and social freedom.

In 2008, Barack Obama became the first African American to be elected President of the United States.

Atlanta Georgia - American Civil War

The city of Atlanta, Georgia, in Fulton County, was an important rail and commercial center during the American Civil War. Atlanta became a critical point of contention during the Atlanta Campaign in 1864 when a powerful Union army approached from Union-held Tennessee.

The fall of Atlanta was a pivotal moment in the Civil War. With the North's confidence and the victories at Mobile Bay and Winchester, lead to the re-election of President Lincoln and the final surrender of the Confederacy.

Gone With The Wind - Burning of Atlanta Georgia

"Like Scarlett O'Hara, we survived the harsh rule of Reconstruction. After a hard thrashing, we pulled ourselves up by our bootstraps and built this region back into one of the most vibrant economies in the world." Mimi Gentry

"I feel like if you're a girl in the South, you know 'Gone with the Wind' better than anything. Scarlett O'Hara is such a quintessential Southern woman." Leslie Bibb

"I became a novelist because of; 'Gone With the Wind.' More precisely, my mother raised me up to be a 'Southern' writer, with a strong emphasis on the word 'Southern' because 'Gone With the Wind.' The movie set my mother's imagination ablaze when she was a young girl growing up in Atlanta." Pat Conroy

We Will Never Forget

"Shows have a tendency to end when they're over. 'The Dukes of Hazzard' has not ended for the fans, and it has not ended for the cast or the crews, and I'm very proud to be a part of that." John Schneider

I am Proud to be a Southern Woman

"I'm very Southern in the way I walk and talk. I love to laugh. I like to eat southern food. I like to hug people. I have friends of all races. I am proud to be a "Southern Woman'. I love our flags and the positives they represent. If somebody makes me mad, my eyes may roll. I can be aggressive with a Southern twang." Rosa Ann Crowder

"If you like good ol' fashion Southern soul food then, yes, I am a good cook! My specialty is chicken dumplings and Poke Salad." Dolly Parton

"For breakfast, I have grits, because I am a Southern girl." Shanola Hampton

Black-eyed Peas

Kudos to the Black-eyed Peas

In celebration of the New Year

This tasty and nourishing vegetable

is placed on every table of the south

In hopes of more money will appear

Its nutty flavor is a satisfying staple

With a robust, delicious dish on the side

As it satisfies taste buds in our mouth

There is no substitute for black-eyed peas

Served with greens and hot cornbread

Sliced onions and tea completes the meal

This vegetable is like the people of the south

We are nutty, robust and try to get ahead

Some of us are resilient and want to squeal

In hopes of our needs will be supplied

We will never have to be or do without

Banana Pudding

Classic Southern Dessert

The old fashioned banana pudding is a style of dessert that has been a favorite for generations — made with a creamy vanilla egg custard - layered with vanilla wafers, slices of bananas, and the custard — then topped with a wavy homemade meringue.

The only tricky part about this vintage delight is waiting for it to cool before eating.

I've always stayed true to that tradition. However, You can use whipped cream instead of meringue, and instant pudding instead of custard. You can't go wrong, either way.

My fascination with banana pudding began at a young age. It was an absolute necessity on the dessert table at every single special event, church social, and extended family gathering.

There were tables arranged with the best of Southern food.

You Will Need

9 X 13 rectangular, deep baking dish

electric hand mixer

whisk

fork

2 mixing bowls

a heavy - deep saucepan

dessert bowls

Prep Time: 20 minutes - Cook Time: 20 minutes - Chill 2 hours

Custard Ingredients:

3 - 12 oz can of evaporated milk

16 ounces of water

1 cup granulated sugar

1/4 cup self-rising flour

7 large egg yolks (reserve egg whites)

3 Tbsp butter

1 Tbsp pure vanilla extract

2 boxes vanilla wafers

6 medium bananas sliced

Instructions:

In a deep mixing bowl - whisk together the evaporated milk, water, granulated sugar, flour, and the egg yolks until mixed. Pour into the deep heavy saucepan.

Cook over medium continuously for about 10 -15 minutes until the custard has thickened. Once thickened remove from the heat. Whisk in the butter and vanilla. Set aside

In a 9 X 13-inch oven safe dish, layer the bottom with vanilla wafers. Top with banana slices. Cover with 1/3 of the custard fillings. Repeat ending with custard.

Meringue Ingredients

7 reserved egg whites

1 tsp pure vanilla extract

6 Tbsp granulated sugar

Instructions:

Preheat the oven at 450 degrees

Mix the 7 egg whites with a mixer, add the vanilla and mix, pour sugar a little at a time while mixing. Beat on high until stiff peaks.

Spread the meringue on top of the banana pudding. Use a fork to make peaks. Place on middle rack in oven for 10 - 15 minutes until golden. Remove from oven and set aside to cool.

Peaches

Peaches are delicious and incredibly healthy fruit to eat. Living in Alabama gives us easy access to delicious peaches from the Georgia peach trees.

We enjoy peaches, and you will find astonishing, great peaches recipes in my cookbooks.

Tips:

Store the peaches in the refrigerator for up to 5 days. It would be best to wash peaches under cold running water to remove any dirt.

If a recipe calls for peeled peaches, dip peaches in boiling water which will loosen the skin and peel right off.

Sprinkle peaches with lemon juice to keep peaches from turning brown.

If your peaches are not ripe enough, place them in room temperature until they are soft enough to eat

Peach Bread

Ingredients:

3/4 cup chopped pecans

2 1/2 cups self-rising flour

1 cup of sugar

1/2 tsp. ground cinnamon

1/4 tsp. ground nutmeg

I 1/2 cups peeled and chopped peaches

3/4 cup freshly grated carrots

2/3 cup canola oil

1/2 cup milk

Two large eggs, lightly beaten

Directions:

Preheat oven to 350 °

Bake pecans in a single layer on a sheet pan 5 to I0 minutes until toasted. Cool 10 minutes.

Stir together dry ingredients; add remaining ingredients and stir until moistened. Spoon batter into 9" x 5" greased cake or loaf pan.

Bake at 350° for 60 minutes

Insert a toothpick in the center, and it should come out clean. Cool in the pan for 5 minutes, then, remove from pan and proceed to cool on a wire rack for about an hour.

Peach Salsa

Ingredients:

Three firm peaches (peeled and diced)

One tablespoon lemon juice

One tablespoon chopped jalapeno peppers

Two ripe tomatoes (peeled and diced)

Four green onions (diced)

One tablespoon Cilantro (chopped)

Five tablespoons extra virgin olive oil

Three tablespoons sherry vinegar

One tablespoon honey

Directions:

Combine the peaches, tomatoes, onions, peppers, and cilantro.

Whisk together oil, vinegar, and honey. Pour over other ingredients and lightly stir.

Peach Pie

Ingredients:

Five cups peaches (peeled and sliced)

1 cup of sugar

3 tbsp. flour

Pinch of salt

2 tbsp. melted salted butter

Two deep dish pie crust

Directions

Grease a deep dish 9-inch pie pan.

Place the bottom crust in a 9-inch pie pan.

Pour peaches on top of the crust.

Sprinkle the sugar and flour on top of the peaches.

 Drizzle the butter on top.

Moisten the edges of the bottom pie crust and place the top piecrust. Gently mash the edges together and trim off the excess. Cut about 12 knife dashes in top piecrust.

Bake 15-17 minutes, at 400°, then reduce heat to 350° and bake another 25 to 30 minutes or until pastry is well browned and juice bubbles up through lattice.

Remove to rack to cool until lukewarm and then serve!

Peach Ice Cream

Ingredients:

Seven very ripe peaches (peeled and diced)

1 cup half-and-half

2 cups of sugar

Two teaspoons vanilla

1/2 gallon milk

Two tablespoons lemon juice

Directions:

Put all ingredients into a 1gallon ice cream maker and stir well. Place the ice cream dasher and lid. Follow the manufacturer's instructions.

Your Recipes

_____

_____

_____

_____

_____

_____

Some of the books written by Rosa Ann Crowder:

Wonder-Woman
Kickass Business Tactics

Inspirational Poems

Rosa's Brunch Recipes

Rosa's Concepts of Life, Love, and Living

Southern & Conservative

rosas.concepts101@gmail.com

https://rosas-concepts.business.site

www.rosas-concepts.com

www.business-solutions-rosas-concepts.com

www.ingramcontent.com/pod-product-compliance
Lightning Source LLC
Chambersburg PA
CBHW070442290526
45791CB00005B/2071